Who Are the Real Winners?

商務印書館（香港）有限公司
http://www.commercialpress.com.hk

CENGAGE
Learning™

Australia • Brazil • Japan • Korea • Mexico • Singapore • Spain • United Kingdom • United States

Who Are the Real Winners? 真正的第一名

Director of Content Development:
Anita Raducanu
Series Editor: Rob Waring
Editorial Manager: Bryan Fletcher

Associate Development Editors:
Victoria Forrester, Catherine McCue
責任編輯：黃家麗

出版：

商務印書館（香港）有限公司
香港筲箕灣耀興道3號東匯廣場8樓

Cengage Learning
Units 808-810, 8th floor,
Tins Enterprises Centre,
777 Lai Chi Kok Road, Cheung Sha Wan,
Kowloon, Hong Kong

網址：http://www.commercialpress.com.hk

http://www.cengageasia.com

發行：香港聯合書刊物流有限公司
　　　香港新界大埔汀麗路36號中華商務
　　　印刷大廈3字樓

印刷：勝利印務私人有限公司
版次：2009年9月第1版第1次印刷

ISBN: 978-962-07-1874-8

出版說明

本館一向倡導優質閱讀，近年連續推出以"Q"為標誌的優質英語學習系列(*Quality English Learning*)，其中《Black Cat 優質英語階梯閱讀》，讀者反應令人鼓舞，先後共推出超過60本。

為進一步推動閱讀，本館引入Cengage 出版之*Footprint Library*，使用*National Geographic*的圖像及語料，編成百科英語階梯閱讀系列，有別於Black Cat 古典文學閱讀，透過現代真實題材，百科英語語境能幫助讀者認識今日的世界各事各物，擴闊視野，提高認識及表達英語的能力。

本系列屬non-fiction (非虛構故事類)讀本，結合閱讀、視像和聽力三種學習功能，是一套三合一多媒介讀本，每本書的英文文章以headwords寫成，headwords 選收自以下數據庫的語料：*Collins Cobuild The Bank of English*、*British National Corpus* 及 *BYU Corpus of American English* 等，並配上精彩照片，另加一張video/audio 兩用DVD。編排由淺入深，按級提升，只要讀者堅持學習，必能有效提高英語溝通能力。

商務印書館(香港)有限公司

編輯部

使用說明

百科英語階梯閱讀分四級，共八本書，是彩色有影有聲書，每本有英語文章供閱讀，根據數據庫如 *Collins Cobuild The Bank of English*、*British National Corpus* 及 *BYU Corpus of American English* 選收常用字詞編寫，配彩色照片及一張video/audio 兩用DVD，結合閱讀、聆聽、視像三種學習方式。

讀者可使用本書：

 學習新詞彙，並透過延伸閱讀(Expansion Reading) 練習速讀技巧

 聆聽錄音提高聽力，模仿標準英語讀音

 看短片做練習，以提升綜合理解能力

Grammar Focus解釋語法重點，後附練習題，供讀者即時複習所學，書內其他練習題，有助讀者掌握學習技巧如 scanning, prediction, summarising, identifying the main idea

中英對照生詞表設於書後，既不影響讀者閱讀正文，又具備參考作用

Contents 目錄

The CD-ROM contains a video and full recording of the text

CD-ROM *包括短片和錄音* ▢ 🎧

Words to Know

This story is set in Thailand.
It happens in and around
Chiang Mai, a city in the north
of Thailand.

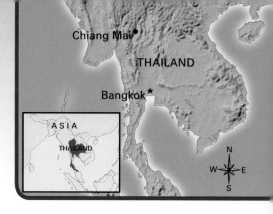

 Thai Boxing. Read the paragraph. Complete the definitions with the correct form of the underlined words.

Thai boxing, or *Muay Thai*, is a traditional martial art from Thailand. It involves a number of special ceremonies. The boxers perform most of these special actions in the boxing ring.
Thai boxers start training when they are very young. They all dream of becoming a champion. Being a Thai boxer gives them a high status in their community. It also makes their families very proud.

1. The _____ is the place where a fight happens.

2. _____ are people who fight for sport.

3. _____ means a special position in society.

4. _____ means pleased or satisfied with a person or action.

5. _____ are events or actions performed on special occasions.

6. _____ refer to traditional Asian skills of fighting.

7. A _____ is the final winner; the best.

Thai Boxers in the Boxing Ring

B **Fighting with the Entire Body.** All of these body parts are used in Thai boxing. Read the definitions. Write the number of the correct underlined word next to each part of the body.

1. The <u>knee</u> is part of the leg. It connects the top of the leg to the bottom of the leg.
2. The <u>elbow</u> is part of the arm. It connects the two parts of the arm.
3. The <u>head</u> is at the top of the body.
4. The <u>feet</u> are at the ends of the legs.
5. The <u>hands</u> are at the ends of the arms.

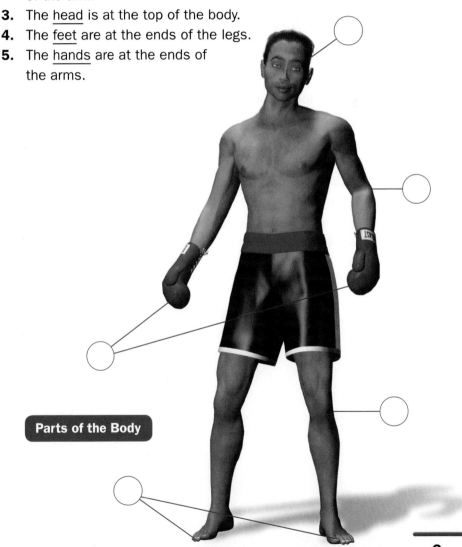

Parts of the Body

Thai boxing, or *Muay Thai*, is Thailand's most ancient martial art. It looks a bit like Western boxing, but it's actually quite different. In Thai boxing, you can use every part of your body: your hands, head, feet, knees – even elbows are allowed.

The sport has a long history. Two thousand years ago, **warriors**[1] trained in Thai boxing to protect their country from **invaders.**[2] Now, it's one of Thailand's most popular sports. Almost everyone in Thailand loves it. It's part of almost every **festival**[3] and it's shown on television around the whole country every day.

---

[1] **warrior:** a fighter
[2] **invader:** a person who enters a country or place by force
[3] **festival:** a day or time when people celebrate a special event

Two thousand years ago, Thai boxing started as a way to protect Thailand. Now, it's a popular sport.

Some of the most successful boxers in Thailand started boxing at the Lanna Muay Thai Training Camp in Chiang Mai. At the moment, the camp is home for a 12-year-old boy called Manat. He and 15 other boys have come here to become boxers.

Most of the boys are young and many come from poor families. The camp pays for their training. While they are here, they do very little except box – all the time. The boys have to train for seven hours a day, seven days a week. They train this hard in the hope of becoming the next great champion. For Manat and the others, success here could lead to better lives and higher **status**[1] in Thai society.

---

[1]**status:** social position

Fact Check: True or false?

1. You can't use your head in Thai boxing.

2. You can see Thai boxing on TV.

3. There are 15 boys at the training camp.

4. The boys come from families with a lot of money.

5. The boys train every day.

The camp was started by a Canadian **coach**[1] called Andy Thomson. Thomson explains why Thai boxing is so important for the boys: 'Thai boxing offers the boys a chance at status … improve[d] status in their community, the **opportunity**[2] to earn some money, and most of them will have a dream of being a champion one day in Lumphini Stadium in Bangkok. It's an opportunity to open up their world.'

For Manat and the other boys, this is their big chance. It's a chance to see more than just their home village. It's also a chance to make their family and friends very proud.

a coach

_____

[1]**coach:** person who teaches and trains sportspeople
[2]**opportunity:** a chance

a Thai boxer

a boxing ring

A Thai Boxing Training Camp

The boys may be dreaming of **success**,[1] but they have a lot of work to do at the moment. Manat is getting ready for his second fight, which will happen tomorrow. He's been practising a lot. Thai boxers have to be strong, but they also must practise very hard. It's not only about training their bodies. They also have to prepare their minds and the way they think about the fight.

---

[1]**success:** the achievement of sth that you planned to do

Modern *Muay Thai* is about even more than just learning to think and fight like a warrior. It's also about achieving a personal goal. Helping his parents and making them proud is very important to Manat. He says: 'If I move on to the bigger fights, one day I'll be a champion – a champion of Chiang Mai. I'll feel very proud and good. And I'll send the money I win to my parents.'

A Thai Boxer prepares for his fight.

Manat's big night finally arrives. The fight is in a small town outside Chiang Mai. Manat goes into the boxing ring for the 'Rama Muay'. This is an ancient ceremony which focuses a fighter's **strength**[1] and power. It helps him to get ready for the fight.

After the ceremony, Manat's important fight finally begins. But what are the **judges**[2] looking for in Manat's **technique**,[3] or style of boxing?

---

[1]**strength:** physical power
[2]**judge:** a person who decides who wins or loses
[3]**technique:** a particular skill to do an activity

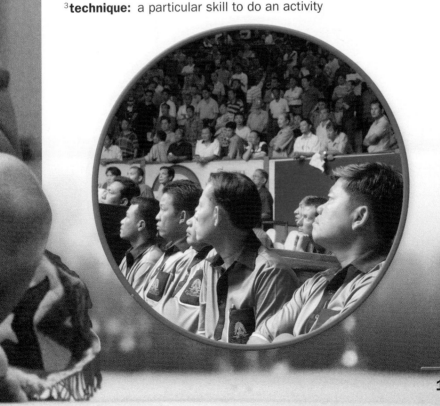

Coach Thomson explains, 'The judges are looking for a good, clean shot technique – both **defensive**[1] and **offensive**.[2] They are looking for the boxer who is in control of the fight,' he says.

Manat fights hard, but for him tonight is not the night. He doesn't win the fight. What went wrong? Why didn't Manat win?

---

[1] **defensive:** protecting oneself or sb from an attack
[2] **offensive:** attacking or hurting sb

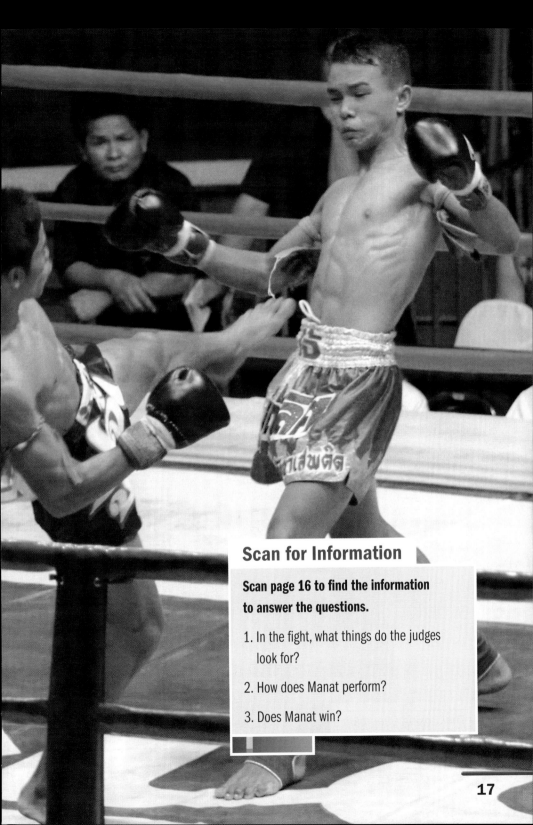

Scan for Information

Scan page 16 to find the information to answer the questions.

1. In the fight, what things do the judges look for?

2. How does Manat perform?

3. Does Manat win?

Thai Boxing Champion
Manus Boonjumnong

Unfortunately, the boy Manat fought was taller, heavier, and more experienced than him. But even with these **disadvantages**,[1] Manat did very well. He may have lost the fight, but his coaches now definitely believe in him. They believe that he can be a winner.

Thomson describes the fight: 'Manat's fight was very good. He fought really well. [He had a] **good attitude** ... a **good heart**[2]... very good heart.' He then adds, 'even though he's not happy, he'll be all right tomorrow. He'll be back fighting again – no problem.'

Manat may not have won this fight, but it's OK. He must remember that tonight's fight was only one step in the long **process**[3] of making a Thai boxing champion.

---

[1] **disadvantage:** sth which makes it harder to succeed
[2] **good attitude/good heart:** good way of thinking/strong will or mind
[3] **process:** a series of actions taken to achieve a result

After You Read

1. What part of your body can you use in Thai boxing?
   A. elbows
   B. hands
   C. head
   D. all of the above

2. On page 4, 'protect' in the second paragraph means:
   A. stop from
   B. take away
   C. keep safe
   D. join together

3. At the training camp, the boys practise:
   A. daily.
   B. sometimes.
   C. never.
   D. occasionally.

4. A good heading for page 6 is:
   A. No Chiang Mai Champions.
   B. Boxing Camp for Rich Boys.
   C. Manat, a Future Champion.
   D. Training is Easy for Boys.

5. Andy Thomson believes that boxing in Thailand:
   A. is better than boxing in Canada.
   B. gives boys a chance for a better life.
   C. is not important.
   D. can make anyone rich.

6. Why does the writer say that Thai boxing is not only about training bodies?
   A. To explain that it's also about training the mind.
   B. To show that Manat must work harder.
   C. To describe Manat's third fight.
   D. To show that boxers must only be strong.

7. Modern Muay Thai is not _____ about learning to think and fight.
   A. at all
   B. really
   C. also
   D. just

8. What does Manat think is good about boxing?
   A. He can live away from home.
   B. He can learn about training.
   C. He can win every time.
   D. He can help his mother and father.

9. The ancient ceremony helps Manat feel prepared to fight.
   A. True
   B. False

10. On page 16, 'they' in the first paragraph refers to:
    A. boxers
    B. coaches
    C. judges
    D. Manat's family

11. What is a good heading for page 19?
    A. Manat Fights Well But Loses
    B. Manat Wins Big Fight
    C. Manat Cannot Box Well
    D. Coach Worries About Boy

12. What does the writer think about Manat's future?
    A. He cannot be a champion.
    B. He is going to be a successful boxer.
    C. He will never be the champion of Chiang Mai.
    D. He will win his next fight.

Kano Jigoro, the Man Who Created Judo

by Julia Park

Japan has a long history of martial arts that started over 2,500 years ago. Many different martial arts have developed since then. In these martial arts, fighters use their hands, feet, knees, elbows, and heads to fight. Ancient history says that Japanese warriors often used martial arts skills to protect their families and country. However, martial arts also had another purpose. They were used to train the mind. A good fighter had to be a skilled thinker.

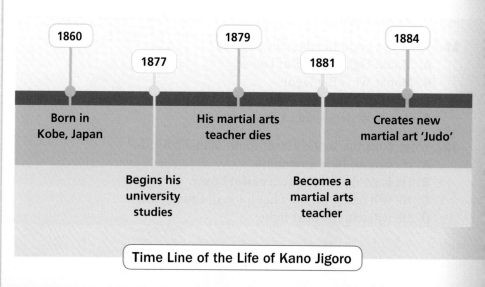

1860		1879		1884
	1877		1881	
Born in Kobe, Japan		His martial arts teacher dies		Creates new martial art 'Judo'
	Begins his university studies		Becomes a martial arts teacher	

Time Line of the Life of Kano Jigoro

Judo involves thinking as well as fighting.

In the late 1800s, the best-known martial art was 'jujitsu'. However, jujitsu was about to experience an important change. A man called Kano Jigoro used his influence to develop a new form of jujitsu. He called this new form 'Judo'.

Kano Jigoro was born in Kobe, Japan, in 1860. When he was a small child, bigger boys would follow him and try to fight with him. One day, Jigoro learned a bit about jujitsu from a friend of his father. Jigoro was immediately interested. When he began his university studies, he also began the serious study of jujitsu. Two years later, his teacher died. He had to find another teacher. By the time he was 21, Jigoro was very good at jujitsu and he had become a teacher himself.

As time passed, he began to develop a new type of martial art. It had many of the characteristics of jujitsu. However, Jigoro added some of his own ideas as well. He was especially interested in the thoughtful and spiritual side. He called this new form 'judo'. The word 'ju' means 'gentle' and 'do' means 'way'. Today millions of men, women, and children all over the world practise judo.

Word Count: 321
Time: _____

Words to Know

This story is set in the African countries of Mali and Mauritania, near the Sahara Desert. It happens in the town of Diafarabe and across the Sahel region.

 Cattle Herding. Read the paragraph. Then match each word or phrase with the correct definition.

The Fulani are a group of people in Africa who raise cattle. Every year, young Fulani herdsmen take their cattle to an arid region near the Sahara Desert. There, they must find places for their cows to graze and get food. They must ensure that their dairy cows remain healthy and produce a lot of milk. It's a difficult job because cattle like a temperate climate, not hot and dry places.

1. cattle _____	**a.** a cow used for producing milk
2. herdsmen _____	**b.** very dry
3. arid _____	**c.** large farm animals kept for their milk or meat
4. graze _____	**d.** not very hot and not very cold
5. dairy cow _____	**e.** eat grass or other plants
6. temperate climate _____	**f.** men or boys who care for groups of animals of the same type

The Arid Sahel Region

B **A Dangerous Journey.** Read about the dangers that the Fulani herdsmen meet. Then write each underlined word or phrase next to the correct definition.

Hyenas come out at night and try to kill the cattle.
There are many mosquitoes which cause dangerous diseases.
Cattle rustlers often try to take away the cattle.
In some places, rebels are trying to take over the area.

1. people who steal cattle: _____

2. insects which bite people and animals: _____

3. wild animals from Africa and Asia that look like
dogs: _____

4. groups who are fighting against the people in power
in a country: _____

A Mosquito

A Hyena

a herd of cattle

a Fulani herdsman

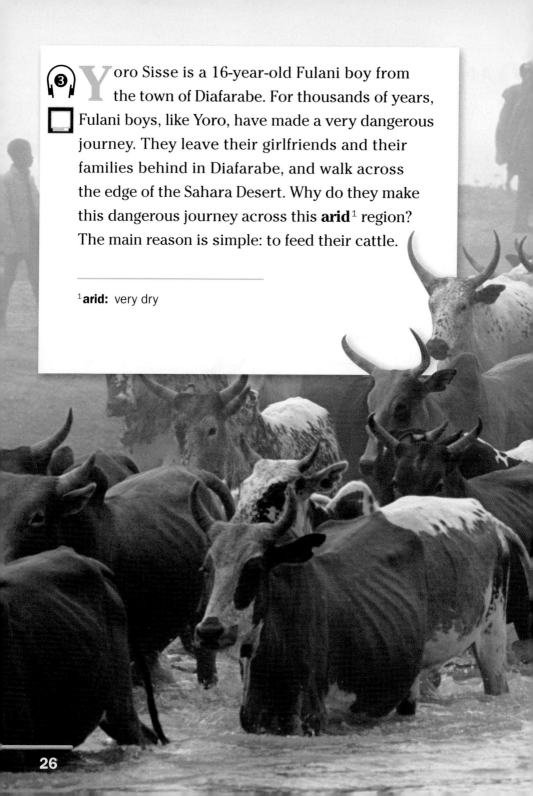

Yoro Sisse is a 16-year-old Fulani boy from the town of Diafarabe. For thousands of years, Fulani boys, like Yoro, have made a very dangerous journey. They leave their girlfriends and their families behind in Diafarabe, and walk across the edge of the Sahara Desert. Why do they make this dangerous journey across this **arid**[1] region? The main reason is simple: to feed their cattle.

[1] **arid:** very dry

Skim for Gist

Read through the entire story quickly to answer the questions.

1. Why is Yoro's success very important?

2. Is Yoro successful on his journey?

At the end of the dry season, Yoro and the other boys must take their cattle out of the **Inner Niger Delta**[1] and into the Sahel. Soon it will be too wet for the cattle in the delta. The herdsmen must travel with their cattle to find better **grazing**[2] areas.

The Sahel is an arid region with very few plants and trees. It goes along the edge of the Sahara Desert, which spreads all the way across Africa. Cattle don't usually live well in arid places. They are animals that like a temperate climate, not dry desert. The success of the Fulani people is a direct result of their ability to raise cattle in an arid **environment**.[3]

---

[1] **Inner Niger Delta:** a low, level land area near the Niger River in Mali
[2] **graze:** to eat grass
[3] **environment:** the surroundings in which one lives

These young cattle herders live away from home with their cattle for up to eight months a year. While they are away, they live mainly on milk that is taken from their dairy cows.

Yoro explains what it's like to make this long and dangerous journey. According to him, the most important thing is to always **be focused on**[1] one thing – grazing. 'We **constantly**[2] have to find new grazing,' he says. 'That's what's always in your mind. In **the bush**,[3] we have to be completely focused. Our **mission**[4] is to bring back fat cattle,' he says. Bringing back fat cattle is very important for Yoro. Why? Because it may determine his future.

---

[1]**be focused on (sth):** have one's attention on one particular thing
[2]**constantly:** all the time
[3]**the bush:** an area of land which has never been farmed
[4]**mission:** main job; goal

For Yoro and other Fulani boys, bringing home a healthy herd is a traditional **rite of passage**.[1] If a Fulani boy returns with healthy cattle, then he is considered to be a man. When Yoro returns home to Diafarabe, the other Fulani people will look carefully at the cattle. They will check his work as a herdsman for the past eight months. They will then decide if he's capable of **managing**[2] a herd properly.

Yoro's girlfriend, Aissa, also hopes that he's done well. She has a good reason for doing so: she's now old enough to get married. In Fulani society, parents choose who their daughters and sons will marry. If Yoro doesn't bring his herd home in **excellent**[3] condition, Aissa's parents probably won't choose him to be her husband.

---

[1] **rite of passage:** an activity which indicates an important stage in a person's life, especially when becoming an adult
[2] **manage:** to keep sb/sth under control
[3] **excellent:** very good

During the journey, Yoro has to make sure that his cattle get enough food in the dry, desert environment. But that's not his only worry. There are also several other dangers. There are **rebels**[1] and **cattle rustlers**.[2] There are also dangerous mosquitoes that can cause serious diseases.

Yoro starts his journey in Diafarabe, Mali, and walks into Mauritania. He follows **routes**[3] that may have existed for thousands of years. They've been here since a time when people and cattle were first forced into the Sahel. As the Sahara region dried out and became a desert, the people that lived there had to leave. They had to find a more temperate climate in which to live.

---

[1] **rebel:** a person who fights a government in their country
[2] **cattle rustler:** a person who steals cattle
[3] **route:** a particular way or direction between places

Yoro walks and walks. Then, after three months in the bush, it's finally time for him to turn and go home. It's been a difficult time for the young boy. 'We walk from sunrise to sunset without stopping,' he says. 'Sometimes we get very thirsty and the cows get tired.' He then adds, 'Often we don't sleep at night.' Why? That's when the **hyenas**[1] come out. They might try to kill the young cows, or 'calves'. Yoro and the other herders often watch their cattle all night. They can't risk losing an animal now!

The last part of Yoro's journey is very difficult. It becomes almost like a forced march for him and the animals. Fortunately, Yoro's herd is doing well. There are many healthy calves and they need to be **branded**.[2] Putting his brand on the calves is a proud moment for Yoro. The calves immediately make his family richer and show Yoro's **courage**[3] and skill during the last eight months.

---

[1]**hyena:** a wild animal that looks like a dog
[2]**brand:** to mark an animal, such as a cow, by burning its skin
[3]**courage:** the ability to control fear in a dangerous or difficult situation

Putting a brand on a calf is a proud moment for Fulani herdsmen.

Yoro is almost home now. He's so close he can almost see it, and he's really excited about seeing his girlfriend, Aissa. There's just one more **challenge**[1] to his long journey. He must cross a dangerous river with his cattle. Yoro's cattle are his future and he wants to be sure of their safety. Because of this, he chooses to cross the river with them.

---

[1] **challenge:** sth that tests one's ability

The cattle mean everything to Yoro. He chooses to cross the river with them to ensure their safety.

After the long journey, Yoro has brought home a healthy herd. Both he and Aissa can be proud of his success. It's time for a happy **celebration**[1] in Diafarabe.

Later, Yoro spends some time with Aissa. He tells her of his **intention**[2] to marry her. Aissa is pleased, but it's Aissa's parents, not Aissa and Yoro, who will decide if they can marry. Yoro has done everything he can. His future, and Aissa's, are linked to the river and the land of the Sahel. They're also linked to the dangerous journey that young Fulani boys have made for thousands of years.

---

[1]**celebration:** a special social event, such as a party, to show that sth is important
[2]**intention:** sth you want and plan to do

Summarise

Summarise the story of Yoro's journey. Write it in a notebook. Include the following information:

· Where did the journey take place?

· Why did he make the journey?

· What were some of the dangers he met?

· How will the journey affect him?

After You Read

1. In the first paragraph on page 26, 'they' refers to:
   A. families
   B. boys
   C. girlfriends
   D. cows

2. Cattle usually prefer a _____ climate to a _____ one.
   A. temperate, dry
   B. cold, wet
   C. dry, cool
   D. hot, wet

3. Match the cause to the effect.
   Effect: Fulani boys take cattle out of the Niger Delta.
   A. People need food in Sahel.
   B. The desert has plants and trees.
   C. The dry season is ending.
   D. Fulani people are good with cattle.

4. The main purpose of Yoro's journey is to:
   A. marry his girlfriend.
   B. make lots of money.
   C. buy new cattle.
   D. return with healthy cattle.

5. The word 'reason' in the second paragraph on page 33 can be replaced by:
   A. cause
   B. decision
   C. care
   D. condition

6. Which of the following is a good heading for page 33?
   A. After Weeks in the Desert
   B. Aissa and Yoro Will Marry
   C. Yoro Must Impress Aissa's Parents
   D. Aissa Won't Marry Yoro

7. Yoro faces many dangers including disease and strong winds.
   A. True
   B. False

8. Yoro's route to Mauritania is:
   A. terrible.
   B. modern.
   C. short.
   D. ancient.

9. On page 36, the word 'march' can be replaced by:
   A. walk
   B. goal
   C. strategy
   D. run

10. The writer probably thinks Yoro is:
   A. nervous.
   B. serious.
   C. hardworking.
   D. lazy.

11. What is a suitable heading for page 38?
   A. Yoro and Cattle Cross Road
   B. Long Journey Finally Begins
   C. A Healthy Herd is Impossible
   D. A Young Man Returns Home

12. What's the purpose of page 40?
   A. to show that Yoro won't marry Aissa
   B. to explain what affects Yoro's future
   C. to teach the importance of listening to parents
   D. to show that Yoro is a special Fulani man

The
BOOK BAG

by Joe and Tina Reed

The Real Cowboy Story

Cowboys have existed in the American west for almost 200 years. Thousands of books have been written about them. Who were the real cowboys and where are they today? Two writers share their views on this interesting subject in their new books. We've read them both and here's what we think.

RATING SCALE
Excellent ★★★★   Terrible ★

Thousands of books have been written about cowboys.

THE FIRST COWBOYS
by Carlos Carrillo, Cowboy Books, $39.95

The first half of Carlos Carrillo's new book seems like a novel. The year is 1600 and three young Spanish men have just arrived in 'New Spain' (what is now Mexico). They have come to be 'vaqueros'. (The exact meaning of this word in English is 'cow men', which later became 'cowboy'.) Carrillo follows Jose, Hector, and Pedro as they learn their skills. They move large herds of cows from place to place, control wild horses, and teach new cowboys everything they know. The second half of the book then describes the historical influence of the *vaqueros* in Mexican and American cultures. It also features some beautiful paintings and pencil drawings. The art and historical descriptions of the second half of the book really support the story in the beginning. Carillo does a great job of bringing the two together.

Interest Level	★★★★	*Art*	★★★
Historical Truth	★★	*Price*	★★

WHERE DID ALL THE COWBOYS GO?
by Rita Turnbell, Gorman Publishing, $12.95

In this carefully researched book, Rita Turnbell explains why there are so few cowboys left today. Before the late 1800s, the western part of the United States was mostly public land. As new Americans moved there to start farms, all the public land disappeared. Soon cowboys were no longer needed. The book explains in detail why the cowboys lost the ability to do their traditional work. It is full of facts and is very good value for money. However, the information could have been presented in a more interesting form. The writer should have given more personal information about the cowboys. She also could have included more artwork to support her points.
This book is an OK read.

Interest Level	★	*Art*	★
Historical Truth	★★★★	*Price*	★★★★

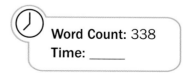

Word Count: 338
Time: _____

Words to Know

This story is set in the United States (U.S.). It happens in San Francisco, California, near the Pacific Ocean.

 A **Taiko Drumming.** Read the paragraph. Then match each word with the correct definition.

Taiko drumming is an ancient Japanese art, but it is also done in Western countries. 'Taiko' is a Japanese word which means 'drum'. These musical instruments make loud noises when taiko drummers beat them. They use drumsticks to do this. Taiko drumming is difficult and the drummers must practise so they can improve. They practise in a special place called a 'dojo'. If a person works very hard, he or she may become a grand master of taiko.

1. drum _____	**a.** hit again and again
2. beat _____	**b.** a stick for hitting a drum
3. drumstick _____	**c.** someone who performs an art at the highest level
4. practise _____	**d.** a Japanese word for 'practice place'
5. *dojo* _____	**e.** do something again and again to get better at it
6. grand master _____	**f.** a round musical instrument hit with hands or sticks

Taiko Drummers

B **In the *Dojo*.** Read the definitions. Complete the paragraph with the correct form of the words.

mind: the part of a person that allows them to think and feel
sensei: Japanese word which means 'teacher'
warrior: fighter
traditional: done for a long time by a particular society or group

Many Japanese arts are practised in a 'dojo'. A *dojo* is a place where people can practise (1)_____ Japanese arts. *Dojos* have a long history. They are the places where many strong Japanese (2)_____ practised and became very good fighters. In a *dojo*, there is always a (3)_____, or teacher, who helps the students improve. The students have to work hard with both their bodies and their (4)_____.

Warriors Fighting in an Ancient Dojo

Two thousand years ago, Japanese warriors used drums to make their **enemies**[1] fear them. In ancient Japan, the drum was very important in everyday life, too. People used to mark village **boundaries**[2] by how far the sounds of drums travelled. People even used to do their daily activities to the beat of drums. However, slowly over the years, the sound of the drums went away – until now.

---

[1]**enemy:** a person or group that wants to hurt another
[2]**boundary:** the point where one thing ends and another begins

Japanese warriors used drums
to make their enemies afraid.

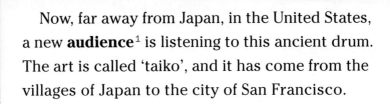

Now, far away from Japan, in the United States, a new **audience**[1] is listening to this ancient drum. The art is called 'taiko', and it has come from the villages of Japan to the city of San Francisco.

One drummer explains an important part of taiko is that a group of **individual**[2] drummers must act as one. 'The **essence**[3] of taiko is that it's not just people drumming,' she says. 'It's the **unity**[4] of drummers amongst themselves.'

---

[1] **audience:** people who come together to listen to and watch an event
[2] **individual:** single
[3] **essence:** basic meaning
[4] **unity:** coming together; feeling of being one

In San Francisco, the movement of the body has now been added to traditional taiko drumming. It is now an art form that brings together sound, body, and mind. During a performance, the **energy**[1] of all of these parts goes into the beating of the drums.

---

[1] **energy:** the power and ability to be active

Identify the Main Idea

1. What is the main idea of the paragraph?

2. What would be a better heading for this page?
   a. 'Traditional Taiko Drumming'
   b. 'Taiko Combines Sound, Body, and Mind'

Some ancient arts have added body movement to bring together sound, body, and mind.

Taiko Grand Master Seiichi Tanaka explains what happens when the drummer and drum unite. According to him, it's almost as if the drum and drummer become one. 'Your self and the drum, totally get together. Into the drum, your self,' he says as he moves his body forward, '... and [the] drum [comes] to you,' he adds as he moves his body back. 'Both [are] **mutual**,[1]' he explains.

---

[1] **mutual:** felt or shared by both

Scan for Information

Scan pages 56-59 to find the information.

1. When did Seiichi Tanaka come to the U.S.?

2. In which two countries did Seiichi Tanaka start taiko drumming?

3. How many groups are there now in the two countries?

In the early 1900s, traditional taiko was very popular in Japanese-American communities. However, by the mid-1900s, many people were losing interest in taiko drumming. Then, in 1968, Seiichi Tanaka arrived and brought new interest and a new style of drumming from Japan. After that, things changed. Tanaka explains: 'I was just **fresh off the boat**,'[1] he says, 'so [a] whole **bunch**[2] of "fresh off the boat" people [got] together and play[ed] drums.'

---

[1]**fresh off the boat:** (*slang*) new to a place or experience
[2]**bunch:** a group

Tanaka is also known as 'Tanaka Sensei' to his students in the *dojo*. They know that he is an important man in taiko. They also realise that he is responsible in part for its popularity in North America. 'Tanaka Sensei is a real **pioneer**,'[1] says one student. 'He's made a dozen or so groups in the sixties and seventies, into something like eight hundred groups now spread all over this country and Canada.'

---

[1] **pioneer:** one of the first people to do sth

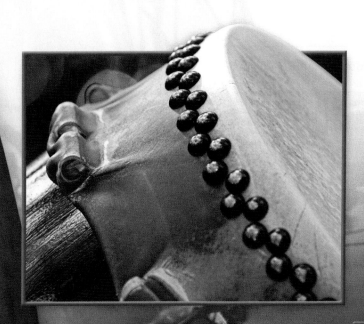

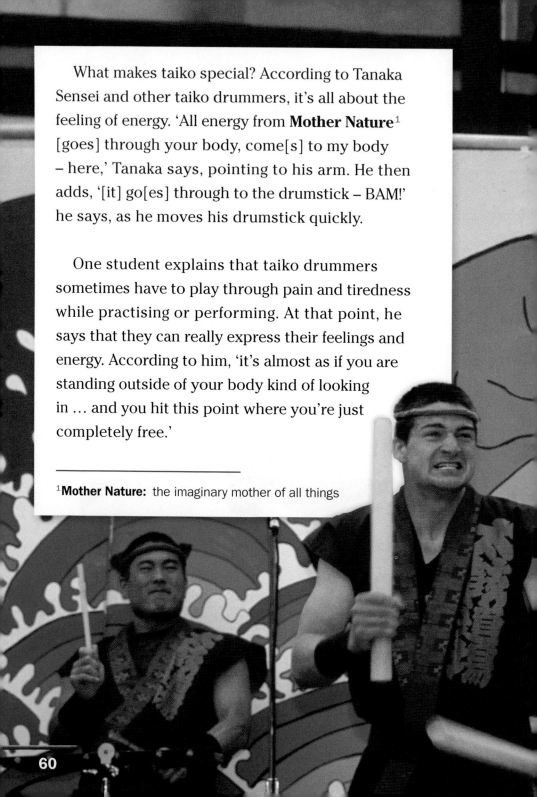

What makes taiko special? According to Tanaka Sensei and other taiko drummers, it's all about the feeling of energy. 'All energy from **Mother Nature**[1] [goes] through your body, come[s] to my body – here,' Tanaka says, pointing to his arm. He then adds, '[it] go[es] through to the drumstick – BAM!' he says, as he moves his drumstick quickly.

One student explains that taiko drummers sometimes have to play through pain and tiredness while practising or performing. At that point, he says that they can really express their feelings and energy. According to him, 'it's almost as if you are standing outside of your body kind of looking in … and you hit this point where you're just completely free.'

_____

[1]**Mother Nature:** the imaginary mother of all things

Another drummer also feels that taiko is about giving energy. 'The essence of taiko is giving your 110 percent,' she says. 'You have to always give, because if you don't give, and everyone else is giving, then you're **draining**[1] from them.'

Here in San Francisco, taiko came from the old world of Japan and was born again. Grand Master Seiichi Tanaka has given North America the chance to enjoy the energy and excitement of traditional taiko drumming.

---

[1]**drain:** take away; use up

After You Read

1. Japanese warriors used their drums to make their enemies:
   A. approach.
   B. fight.
   C. leave.
   D. mark.

2. On page 48, the word 'mark' can be replaced by:
   A. touch
   B. want
   C. research
   D. determine

3. On page 51, the drummer believes that an important part of taiko is:
   A. the group experience.
   B. the individual drummers.
   C. the ancient drums.
   D. the audience.

4. The new form of taiko is from San Diego.
   A. True
   B. False

5. On page 52, 'it' refers to:
   A. movement
   B. sound
   C. the new form of taiko
   D. tradition

6. Sound, _____, and _____ are brought together in this new form of taiko.
   A. tradition, beating
   B. body, mind
   C. performance, mind
   D. body, energy

7. How do the drummer and drum become one?
   A. The energy of playing brings them together.
   B. The drum touches the drummer.
   C. Seiichi Tanaka unites with the drum.
   D. The movement brings together all drummers.

8. What's the main idea on page 56?
   A. Drumming on boats.
   B. Traditional taiko came from the U.S.
   C. Tanaka brought a new drumming style.
   D. People aren't interested in taiko.

9. On page 59, 'sixties and seventies' refers to:
   A. the number of drummers
   B. the time between 1960 and 1979
   C. the age of the drummers
   D. the number of drums

10. Tanaka Sensei thinks that taiko drumming is special because of the:
    A. energy.
    B. drumsticks.
    C. imaginary drums.
    D. Japanese drums.

11. Taiko drummers have to play through _____ and _____.
    A. energy, freedom
    B. pain, expression
    C. pain, tiredness
    D. energy, tiredness

12. What is the purpose of this story?
    A. to introduce the grand masters of Japan
    B. to talk to drummers about old and new taiko
    C. to present old and new Japan
    D. to introduce an energetic drumming style

Scotland's African Drum Village

Most people think of Scotland as a quiet place with fields and farm animals, but did you know that Scotland has a lot more to offer? In recent years, Dundee, Scotland's fourth-largest city, has become a centre for the arts. Few people think of Scotland as a place to hear African drumming. However, just north of Dundee, there is an African drumming programme that attracts a large audience. People come to this event from all over the world.

．．．．．．．．．．．．．．．．．．．．．．．．．．．．．．．．．．．．．

African Drum Village is a five-day meeting between drummers and people who enjoy the excitement of drumming. It is the first and only meeting of its kind in Scotland. Some of the best drummers

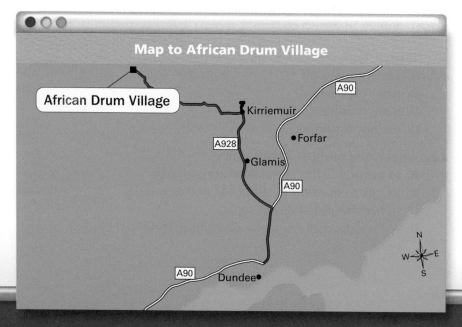

Map to African Drum Village

African Drum Village

Kirriemuir

A90

Forfar

A928

Glamis

A90

A90

Dundee

N
W E
S

in the world attend the programme. There is something for everyone at African Drum Village. As a visitor, you can listen to wonderful performances from grand masters. Beginners can also have drumming lessons with the masters. More experienced drummers can form drumming groups with others. African Drum Village is a spiritual event for many visitors. It is their chance to connect with nature and discover new music. The beauty of Scotland and the skill of the drummers ensure that visitors have a wonderful experience.

This year musician and teacher Famoudou Konaté is the main attraction at African Drum Village. Mr. Konaté is a grand master of drumming in the ancient Malinké Djembe tradition. He was born in 1940 in Guinea in Africa. By the time he was 14 years old, his drumming was already known throughout Africa. For the last 40 years, Konaté has performed in Europe, the United States, and many other parts of the world. African Drum Village is very pleased to present Mr. Konaté this year.

A Visitor Enjoying African Drum Village

Word Count: 326
Time: _____

Grammar Focus: Modals of Necessity: have to, must

■ Modals of necessity are followed by the base form of the verb.
Must/have to express the idea 'this is necessary'.
Not have to expresses the idea 'this is not necessary'.
Must not expresses the idea 'this is not allowed'.

	have	train	every day.
Boxers	don't have to	be	Thai.
	must	have	a good attitude.
	must not	be	lazy.

Grammar Practice: Modals of Necessity: have to, must

Read the sentences and circle the correct modal verb.

e.g. Thai boxers (*must*/mustn't) learn to use all parts of their body in a fight.

1. You (have to/don't have to) be Thai to be a coach in Thai boxing.

2. Thai boxers (must/don't have to) perform special ceremonies before a fight.

3. Boys at the training camp (must not/have to) practise boxing every day.

4. Thai boxers (have to/don't have to) listen carefully to the coach.

5. At my school, students (must/don't have to) wear a uniform.

6. In our class, students (don't have to/must not) forget their English homework.

Grammar Focus: Passive: Present and Past

■ The passive voice can be used with any verb tense. In the present tense, it is formed with *am/is/are* plus the past participle. In the simple past, it is formed with *was/were* plus the past participle.

■ Sentences in the passive voice focus on the result of the action, not the person who does the action (the agent).

■ The agent is mentioned in the sentence only if that information is important. Use *by* + agent.

	be	past participle		agent
I	am (not)	paid	twice a month.	(by my employer)
Yogurt	is (not)	made	from milk.	
Cattle	are (not)	taken	into the Sahel.	(by Fulani men)
The president	was (not)	elected	in October.	
These dishes	were (not)	given to me		(by my grandmother)

■ Grammar Practice: Passive: Present and Past

Circle the correct form of the verb.

e.g. As a child, I (am/(was)) told to go to bed early.

1. Now, I (am/was) given a choice about when to go to bed.

2. A Fulani husband (is/was) always chosen by the woman's parents.

3. When the prince and princess got married, they (are/were) given a beautiful castle.

4. An early form of writing (is/was) invented by the Egyptians around 3,000 BC.

5. Nowadays, computers (are/were) used in almost every kind of business.

69

Grammar Focus: Questions with the Passive Voice

■ Questions with the passive voice are formed by inverting the usual order of the subject and the appropriate form of the verb *to be*.

'Wh' word	be	subject	past participle		agent
	Was	wheat	grown	in ancient Egypt?	(by farmers)
	Are	cattle	given	names?	
What	is	yogurt	made	from?	
Why	were	Yoro's calves	branded?		(by him)

Grammar Practice: Questions with the Passive Voice

Unscramble the words in parentheses to make questions. Then write down the answers.

e.g. (Was/Yoro/for/away/months/eight)
   Was Yoro away for eight months?   Yes.

1.   (When/taken/the Sahel/cattle/are/into)

   _____

2.   (How often/country/held/are/elections/in/your)

   _____

3.   (Are/your/used/in/chopsticks/country)

   _____

4.   (What/used/aspirin/is/for)

   _____

Grammar Focus: Reflexive Pronouns

■ Reflexive pronouns are used when the subject and the object in a sentence are the same person or thing.

I		myself	
You		yourself	
She	saw	herself	in the mirror.
He		himself	
It		itself	

You		yourselves	
They	saw	themselves	in the mirror.
We		ourselves	

Grammar Practice: Reflexive Pronouns

Fill in the blanks with the correct reflexive pronoun: ~~myself~~, *yourself, themselves, herself, ourselves.*

e.g. I wrote a note to ___*myself*___ because I didn't want to forget.

1. They looked at _____ in the large store window.
2. We do some things for our parents and some things for _____.
3. You have to tell _____ that you can do well in the test.
4. She didn't give _____ enough time to enjoy her lunch.

Video Practice

A. Watch the entire video of *Making a Thai Boxing Champion* and circle the word you hear.

1. 'It looks a bit like Western boxing, but it's actually quite (different/special).'
2. 'They train this hard in the hope of becoming the next (big/great) champion.'
3. 'For Manat and the other boys, this is their chance to see more than just their home (town/village).'
4. 'Modern Muay Thai is about even more than just (trying/ learning) to think and fight like a warrior.'
5. 'After the ceremony, the fight finally (starts/begins).'
6. 'Manat fights hard, but for him, (tonight/this) is not the night.'

B. Watch the video again and fill in the word you hear.

1. 'It's part of almost every festival and it's shown on television around the whole country every _____.'
2. 'Most of the boys are young and they come from very _____ families.'
3. 'It's also a chance to make their family and _____ very proud.'
4. 'Manat is getting ready for his second fight. It's going to happen _____.'
5. 'Unfortunately, the boy Manat fought was taller, _____, and more experienced than him.'
6. 'He may have lost the fight, but his coaches now definitely believe that he can be a _____.'

Video Practice

C. Watch the entire video of *One Boy's Journey* and mark **T** (True) or **F** (False).

    1. _____ All of Yoro's cattle are brown.

    2. _____ The Fulani men use a gun to make the hyenas run away.

    3. _____ The video shows Aissa holding a baby.

D. Watch the video again and complete the sentences with the correct words.

    1. 'At the end of the dry season, the boys must take their _____ out of the Inner Niger Delta and into the Sahel.'

    2. 'Cattle like a _____ climate.'

    3. 'The success of the Fulani people is a direct result of their ability to raise cattle in this _____ environment.'

    4. 'While they're away, they live mainly on milk that is taken from their _____ cows.'

    5. 'There are rebels, cattle rustlers, and dangerous _____ that can cause serious diseases. '

E. Watch the video again and answer the questions.

    1. How many months has Yoro been away for when he turns around to go home? _____

    2. How does Yoro feel when he brands his calves? _____

    3. What is the last challenge Yoro faces on this journey? _____

    4. What do the people of Diafarabe do when the herdsmen return? _____

    5. How does Aissa feel when Yoro tells her he wants to marry her? _____

Video Practice

F. Read the sentences. Then watch the video of *Taiko Master* and circle the word you hear.

1. 'Slowly over (time/the years), the sound of the drums went away …'
2. 'The (art/music) is called "taiko", and it has come from the villages of Japan to the city of San Francisco.'
3. 'The essence of taiko is that it's not just (individuals/people) drumming.'
4. 'During a performance, the energy of all of these parts goes into the (playing/beating) of the drums.'
5. 'Then, in 1968, Seiichi Tanaka arrived and brought a new interest and a new style of (drumstick/drumming) from Japan.'

G. Watch the video again and match the phrases to make correct sentences.

1. By the mid-1900s _____
2. Tanaka is also known as _____
3. Tanaka's students _____
4. The feeling of energy _____
5. A drummer says that _____

a. makes taiko special.
b. know he is an important man in taiko.
c. many people were losing interest in traditional taiko drumming.
d. Tanaka Sensei.
e. it's also about giving energy.

(1) Thai boxers begin their training when they are very young. (2) Many of them leave home at the age of 12 to join other boxing students at a training camp. (3) At the camp, they practise the skills they will need to become champions. (4) They must learn to think and fight like warriors. (5) This means developing a good attitude as well as a strong body. (6) At the camps, the boys train seven hours a day, seven days a week. (7) There are many reasons why boys want to become boxers. (8) Some want to have a chance to see more of the world than just their home village. (9) Others want to improve their status in society. (10) Many want their parents and friends to be proud of them. (11) They also want to make money so that they can help their families have a better life. (12) Unfortunately, these boys miss some important childhood years with their families.

A. Read the paragraph and answer the questions.

1. What is a good heading for this paragraph?
   A. Building a Strong Body and Mind
   B. Making Money by Boxing
   C. How and Why Boys Become Thai Boxers
   D. Why Thai Boxers Start Young

2. Thai Boxers _____.
   A. don't think about making money
   B. usually stay in their home villages
   C. don't have to be strong
   D. learn their skills in training camps

3. Thai boxers train _____.
   A. seven days a week
   B. eight hours a day
   C. five days a week
   D. ten hours a day

4. The word 'many' in sentence 10 refers to _____.
   A. parents
   B. friends
   C. boys
   D. families

5. The writer _____.
   A. thinks the boys don't care about their families
   B. thinks the boys shouldn't leave home when they are so young
   C. wants the boxers to make more money
   D. thinks the training is too difficult

6. Where should this sentence go? They never have a day when they don't have to practise.
   A. after sentence 2
   B. after sentence 5
   C. after sentence 6
   D. after sentence 8

B. Answer the questions.

7. An event or action performed on a special occasion is a _____.
A. ceremony
B. status
C. champion
D. proud

8. The _____ connects the two parts of the arm.
A. foot
B. head
C. elbow
D. head

9. In order to develop strong bodies, Thai boxers _____ exercise every day.
A. have to
B. don't have to
C. must not
D. has to

10. Decide which underlined word is incorrect.

Boxers <u>have</u> <u>to</u> be strong so
      A **B**
they <u>must</u> <u>to</u> practise a lot every
     C **D**
day.

(1) Yoro is a boy from the Fulani town of Diafarabe. **(2)** He is 16 years old. **(3)** At the end of the dry season, he and some other boys his age leave Diafarabe and take their cattle to the Sahel region. **(4)** Yoro has to be sure that the cattle get enough to eat in this hot, dry area so that they stay healthy and produce a lot of milk. **(5)** Unfortunately, the climate is not the only possible danger. **(6)** Yoro also has to protect his cows from the hyenas and the cattle rustlers in the area. **(7)** There are mosquitoes which can cause dangerous diseases, so he has to protect himself as well. **(8)** After eight months of travelling, Yoro is now returning home. **(9)** This involves one final challenge. **(10)** He has to guide his cattle across a dangerous river. **(11)** Finally he gets home, and the people of Diafarabe look at his cattle carefully. **(12)** The animals all look strong and healthy and so Yoro is considered to be a man, not a boy. **(13)** Now he is free to marry his girlfriend, Aissa.

A. Read the paragraph and answer the questions.

11. What is the purpose of this paragraph?
  A. to show how rustlers steal cattle
  B. to explain why cattle are so important to the people of Diafarabe
  C. to describe the challenges faced by Yoro
  D. to explain how to keep cattle strong and healthy

12. The town of Diafarabe is _____.
  A. inhabited by the Fulani people
  B. in a hot, dry area
  C. in the desert
  D. in the Sahel region

13. Which is the best heading for this paragraph?
  A. Escaping Cattle Rustlers
  B. A Trip to the Sahel Region
  C. Avoiding Dangerous Diseases
  D. Yoro Gets Married

14. According to the paragraph, the cattle look strong and healthy, so _____.
  A. Yoro feels very proud
  B. the villagers consider Yoro to be a man
  C. Yoro will make another trip to the Sahel region this year
  D. they will be killed for their meat

15. What is the best definition of 'graze'?
  - **A.** try to take away cattle
  - **B.** eat grass or plants
  - **C.** try to take over an area
  - **D.** fight against people in power in a country

16. Where should this sentence go?
At this time of year, the water is very deep.
After sentence _____.

B. Answer the questions.

17. Which underlined word is incorrect?
During last <u>year's</u> journey, <u>the</u> cattle <u>are</u> <u>protected</u> from hyenas every night.
  - **A.** year's
  - **B.** the
  - **C.** are
  - **D.** protected

18. Which underlined word is incorrect?
Even today, <u>young</u> boys in Diafarabe <u>were</u> <u>asked</u> to <u>take</u> cattle to the Sahel every year.
  - **A.** young
  - **B.** were
  - **C.** asked
  - **D.** take

C. Read the sentences. Write 'True' or 'False'. Refer to the paragraph if necessary.

19. The word 'this' in sentence 9 refers to protecting himself. _____

20. The word 'arid' means very dry. _____

(1) Seiichi Tanaka is an important taiko teacher. **(2)** People in many countries know who he is. **(3)** He teaches taiko drumming in San Francisco, California. **(4)** Tanaka came to the United States in 1968 and started his own drumming group. **(5)** Today there are around 800 drumming groups in the U.S. and Canada. **(6)** According to Tanaka, what makes taiko drumming special is the way the drummers use their energy. **(7)** He says that the energy comes from Mother Nature, which goes through the drummer's body, and comes out through the drum stick. **(8)** A taiko student explains that sometimes drummers are tired or in pain. **(9)** He says that they can express these feelings through their drumming. **(10)** Another student says, 'The essence of taiko is giving your 110 percent … if you don't give and everyone else is giving, then you're draining [energy] from them.'

A. Read the paragraph and answer the questions.

21. Seiichi Tanaka _____.
  A. came to the United States in 1968
  B. is a drumming student
  C. lives and works in Japan
  D. was born in the United States

22. Seiichi Tanaka _____.
  A. is very young
  B. spends a lot of time in Canada
  C. doesn't want students to express their feelings
  D. is famous

23. The purpose of this paragraph is to _____.
  A. describe the life of Seiichi Tanaka
  B. show how to start a taiko group
  C. explain what is special about taiko
  D. show the steps in learning taiko drumming

24. How many drumming taiko groups are there in the United States and Canada?
  A. about a hundred
  B. about five hundred
  C. about eight hundred
  D. about a thousand

25. Where does this sentence go?
Later, he also helped start several more taiko groups.
  A. after sentence 2
  B. after sentence 4
  C. after sentence 7
  D. after sentence 9

26. The word 'their' in sentence 6 refers to _____.
  A. drums
  B. drummers
  C. drumming groups
  D. drum sticks

B. Answer the questions.

27. A _____ is a fighter.
    A. dojo
    B. sensei
    C. grand master
    D. warrior

28. The part of a person that allows them to think and feel is their _____.
    A. mind
    B. beat
    C. tradition
    D. practice

29. I met a famous sensei yesterday and he introduced _____ to me.
    A. myself
    B. itself
    C. himself
    D. ourselves

30. Decide which underlined word is incorrect.
    If you <u>want</u> something done <u>correctly</u>, you <u>should</u> do it <u>itself</u>.
          A   **B**   **C**   **D**

Key 答案

Making a Thai Boxing Champion

Words to Know: A. 1. boxing ring **2.** Boxers **3.** Status **4.** Proud
5. Ceremonies **6.** Martial arts **7.** champion **B.** [Clockwise from top]
3 (head), 2 (elbow), 1 (knee), 4 (feet), 5 (hands)

Fact Check: 1. False **2.** True **3.** False **4.** False **5.** True

Scan for Information 1. The judges are looking for both defensive and offensive techniques. **2.** He fights hard. **3.** No, he doesn't.

After You Read: 1. D **2.** C **3.** A **4.** C **5.** B **6.** A **7.** D **8.** D **9.** A **10.** C **11.** A **12.** B

One Boy's Journey

Words to Know: A. 1. c **2.** f **3.** b **4.** e **5.** a **6.** d **B. 1.** cattle rustlers
2. mosquitoes **3.** hyenas **4.** rebels

Skim for Gist: (suggested answers) **1.** If Yoro is successful, his girlfriend's parents may choose Yoro to be her husband. **2.** Yes, Yoro returns with healthy cattle and many new calves.

Summarise: open answers

After You Read: 1. B **2.** A **3.** C **4.** D **5.** A **6.** C **7.** B **8.** D **9.** A **10.** C **11.** D **12.** B

Taiko Master

Words to Know: A. 1. f **2.** a **3.** b **4.** e **5.** d **6.** c **B. 1.** traditional
2. warriors **3.** sensei **4.** minds

Identify the Main Idea: (suggested answers) **1.** Taiko drumming in San Francisco is an art form that includes sound, body, and mind
2. b

Scan for Information: 1. in 1968 **2.** the United States and Canada
3. around 800 groups

After You Read: 1. C **2.** D **3.** A **4.** B **5.** C **6.** B **7.** A **8.** C **9.** B **10.** A **11.** C **12.** D

Grammar Practice

Modals of Necessity: 1. don't have to 2. must 3. have to 4. have to 5. open answer 6. must not

Passive: Present and Past: 1. am 2. is 3. were 4. was 5. are

Questions with the Passive Voice: 1. When are cattle taken into the Sahel? 2. How often are elections held in your country? 3. Are chopsticks used in your country? 4. What is aspirin used for?

Reflexive Pronouns: 1. themselves 2. ourselves 3. yourself 4. herself

Video Practice

A. 1. different 2. great 3. village 4. learning 5. begins 6. tonight
B. 1. day 2. poor 3. friends 4. tomorrow 5. heavier 6. winner
C. 1. F 2. F. 3. T **D.** 1. cattle 2. temperate 3. arid 4. dairy
5. mosquitoes **E.** 1. three months 2. proud 3. (crossing) the river
4. They have a celebration. 5. pleased/happy **F.** 1. the years 2. art
3. people 4. beating 5. drumming **G.** 1. c 2. d 3. b 4. a 5. e

Exit Test

1. C 2. D 3. A 4. C 5. B 6. C 7. A 8. C 9. A 10. D 11. C 12. A 13. B
14. B 15. B 16. 10, ten 17. C 18. B 19. False 20. True 21. A 22. D
23. C 24. C 25. B 26. B 27. D 28. A 29. C 30. D

English - Chinese Vocabulary List 中英對照生詞表

(Arranged in alphabetical order)

arid	乾旱的	**hyena**	鬣狗/土狼
audience	聽眾	**individual**	個別的
be focused on (sth)	專注於	**Inner Niger Delta**	尼日爾河內三角洲
boundary	邊界	**intention**	意向
brand	打烙印	**invader**	入侵的人
bunch	一群	**judge**	裁判
cattle rustler	偷牛賊	**manage**	管理
celebration	慶祝活動	**mission**	任務
challenge	挑戰	**Mother Nature**	大自然
coach	教練	**mutual**	共同的
constantly	時常地	**offensive**	攻擊
courage	勇氣	**opportunity**	機會
defensive	防禦	**pioneer**	先驅
disadvantage	不利	**process**	過程
drain	耗盡	**rebel**	叛徒
enemy	敵人	**rite of passage**	人生大事
energy	能量	**route**	路線
environment	環境	**status**	地位
essence	精髓	**strength**	體力
excellent	極佳	**success**	成功
festival	節日	**technique**	技術
fresh off the boat	新手	**the bush**	未開墾的荒野地區
good attitude/ good heart	良好的比賽態度/ 堅定的決心	**unity**	團結
graze	食草	**warrior**	武士